A Guide to Bees

LIL WOLFIE

ISBN: 1515043142
ISBN-13: 978-1515043140

DEDICATION

To all of the honey bees that chase me whenever I go for a walk.

CONTENTS

INTRODUCTION   1

1   The Castes of Bees   4

2   The Bee Colony   7

3   The New Queen Bee   15

4   Forming a New Colony   18

5   The Life Cycle of the Bee   21

6   About the Authot   26

INTRODUCTION

This guide has been created to help you gain an understanding about bees. Hopefully it will encourage you to do your own research, join a club, and perhaps starting taking care of your own hive. For the betterment of bees, for the betterment of the earth.

What are Bees?

Most people see bees as any yellow and black striped, thin winged insects. This is both true and untrue. Bees are insects with paper thin wings, though not all of them are yellow and black striped. Furthermore, not all yellow and black striped insects are bees.

Bees are a specific variety of monophyletic arthropods closely related to wasps and ants. That's right, wasps are not bees. Nor are hornets. One distinct difference between bees and wasps are the little bits of fur on the bee. Wasps tend to have shiny outer exoskeletons, without the added fuzz.

What do they do?

Different types of bees do different jobs, but in general most bees are pollinators. This means they help to pollinate various plants by landing on them and spreading the pollen to other plants.

In fact, bees are the most effective pollinators out of all other pollinators. Their bodies are literally made to more efficiently move pollen around. Part of this has to do with their fur, but they have other physical modifications too.

It's because of this that there is currently such a large effort to save the bees from the recent beedemic. Without bees, many plants would die.

Bees do more than pollinate plants, however.

Bees collect pollens and nectars to feed the hive. They are very big on taking care of the group, so they spend a lot of time keeping things in order. They actually also clean their hives and spend a lot of time taking care of their young offspring.

Of course, bees also make honey. This is what they are most known for. In fact, honeybees in particular are the bees that make excess honey from the pollens and nectars.

They also make a thing known as beeswax, which is used in a lot of products ranging from edibles to beauty to cleaning. Bees actually use this stuff to form the walls of the honeycomb that they put the honey into.

Where are they from?

Bees are from, well, a really long time ago. Bees are distant relatives of the wasp and they had a common ancestor found in a couple different fossils. Most recently was a fossil found of the genus Melittosphex, which is considered "an extinct lineage of pollen-collecting Apoidea sister to the modern bees." The fossil actually dates from sometime in the early Cretaceous period, ~100 mya.

The change from a wasp form to a bee may have come about when the wasp larvae ate pollinator type insects still covered in pollen, thus introducing that food item into their digestive system.

Bees were first found in Africa, and South and Southeast Asia. It wasn't until the form A. Mellifera was introduced to Europe that the honeybee was found anywhere else. In fact, A. Mellifera is the only domesticated species of honey bee to really be brought to various other countries.

How did Beekeeping Begin?

It is unknown exactly when, where, or how beekeeping originated but it appears to have been somewhere in Ancient Egypt around the first dynasty. During this time, there was a title given to a person who took care of the honey. This title was "Sealer of the Honey." It is evident that the role was relatively important. Unfortunately, no actual hives have been found dating during this time period.

Thus we move on to later in Lower Egypt where there was irrigation and many blooming flowers and plants. The bee was chosen as the country's symbol and kings were called bees. Though they kept domesticated bees, they loved wild honey more so they had special people whose job it was to find wild colonies and harvest some of their honey.

How it was spread later is also pretty much unknown, but it is mostly assumed that travelers and traders moved the bees around. There were many successful and unsuccessful attempts to keep bees by various peoples.

There was a failed attempt in Mesopotamia by the governor of Mari and Suhu around 760 BCE. There were about 30 intact hives uncovered in Jerusalem dated around 900 BCE. It was an incredibly widespread thing. In fact, the bees have been spread to every continent and live everywhere except Antarctica and the very furthest Southern and Northern latitudes.

Honeybees are not native to Canada or really anywhere in the Americas, but they were brought over by Europeans settlers of the time. Native Americans called them "white man's flies."

THE CASTES OF BEES

This book will focus on honey bees and honey bee types because those are the bees that one can keep. Each type of bee has different classes. In the case of the honey bee, it was three. They are the male drone, the female worker, and the queen. By the name you would think that the queen has all the power and she does have a lot but it is the worker bees that really dictate how things are run.

All honeybees have two sets of clear, paper thin little wings on their backs. The front set is bigger than the back. They lack stripes on the segment between their belly and their head as well as on their thorax. They have six shiny, black segmented legs, and a little pollen basket in between their hind legs where they collect pollen.

The differences come with the different kinds of honeybees.

The Male Drones

The males in honey bee hives are known as drones. They have very little to do with the hive and their biggest role is making sure queen bees have fertilized eggs. They are technically speaking the lowest ranking bees in this sort of hierarchal structure.

Drones are more plump than both the worker bee and the queen bee. They are almost the shape of what most people know as the common bumble bee. Another distinct difference in the male drone is that its eyes meet at the very top of its head. Yet possibly the biggest dissimilarity is the fact that these male drones do not have stingers, definitely unlike the worker bees and the queen who do actually have stingers.

The Female Worker Bees

The worker bees are the bees you are most likely seeing whenever it is that you see honey bees, or really any kind of bee. They are small. In fact, most of them are between 0.4 to 0.6 in (5 to 15 mm.) This means that they are definitely smaller than the queen. They're also rounder, though a lot less bumblebee shaped than the drones.

The female worker bees are not sexually developed and thus can't create bees like themselves, but they do have a nasty stinger so beware. Actually it's a misconception that worker bees sting just because. They only sting if they feel threatened. So the only time you should be concerned is if you are causing them harm.

The female worker bees have many, many roles. The main ones are cleaning cells and capping cells, attending the queen and tending the brood, receiving nectar from forages, foraging themselves, cleaning away various debris, packing the pollen, building the comb that holds the honey, doing orientation flights, and guarding the hive from thief bees and other various predators.

These bees are the majority of the hive population and that's good because they do a great job at providing for themselves and one another.

The Queen Bee

She is larger and sleeker than all the other bees. It's almost as if she was fed something special to get her that way... Actually she was. She was fed the special food that workers reserve only for queen bees.

A queen bee is always bigger on all ways than the other bees in the hive. If you still can't find her, she has many other distinguishing characteristics. Worker bees have a barb on their stinger that pulls it out when they sting someone. The queen bee has no such barb and thus can sting many times in a row with no problem.

Her abdomen also happens to be a little pointed and her legs a little splayed. If you still can't tell your queen bee, or you're not sure, see how the other bees act around it. A healthy queen has many happy subservient workers.

The Queen is also a special bee because she is the only fertile one of the bunch. This is because a queen's main job is to provide offspring for the lot of them. She goes on mating flights in search of other drones in order to mate with them and provide a new generation of bees for the hive.

Queens also regulate the hive's activities by producing chemicals that guide the behavior of the other bees. So she is the backbone of the society of bees, and the workers are the members of that society that keep each other together. They work together to provide a good and healthy environment.

THE BEE COLONY

A bee colony is generally made up of anywhere from 20,000 to 60,000 female workers, 0 to 1,000 males, and one queen who can live anywhere from 3 to 4 years.

The nest itself is made up of little combs, which are about 25mm wide. The combs are made of little hexagonal cells of which there are three main kinds. The first are the drone cells. These are used only for rearing the male drones. The second are the queen cells which are rarely used and when they are, it's for rearing baby queens.

The third kind of cells have the most use. These are the worker bee cells. They are used for storing pollen and honey as well as for rearing the little new worker bees.

What are the roles of the bees?

The general survival of the colony is all based on how well the workers stick to their roles and work together.

The Female Worker Bees have possibly the most roles out of all the bees. The worker bees make pretty much all of the decisions and essentially they control the hive. The queen who lays the eggs is told by the workers where to lay her eggs and also what kind of eggs to lay. They do this by constructing the specific kinds of cells they need and then nudge the queen over to these cells. It is the shape and structure of the cell that determines what kind of bee hatches, that and what they are fed.

Besides all of this, worker bees also do a lot of housekeeping and feeding. Calling them worker bees is pretty accurate, as they essentially do all of the work.

- Building and Capping Honey Comb – Beeswax is what they make the honey combs out of. To make beeswax they hang themselves upside down and let their digestive systems change their honey into beeswax and energy. From there they manipulate the comb away from their leg spindles and into the comb cells. The wax hardens very quickly and bees have to eat a lot of honey and nectar in order to create it. Then they cap the cells with more beeswax and move on to the next ones.

- Cleaning – There are a lot of things for the female worker bee to clean. First they clean all of the debris off of themselves when they hatch. Before they leave their comb, they give themselves a nice grooming and then emerge to join the others. Next, she starts to clean the various brooding cells. She makes sure that all of these cells are free from any debris or mess before the queen comes and lays her eggs into them. If the queen doesn't think the cell is clean enough, she won't lay her eggs there. The worker bees also clean out any dead invaders or bees, or take out any other random material that has made its way into the cell.

- Keeping the Hive Ventilated – This tends to depend on the temperature of the hive. Ventilation happens when it is very warm out and so some bees go out and fan air into the hive, circulating air. This is especially important so that they might cure the honey. However, when the temperature is cold most bees crowd together for warmth.

- Guard Duty and Executions – One of the more intriguing roles of the worker bee is its soldier-like duties. For guard duty the bee, at its most energetic moment, goes outside the hive and guards the entrance which is where most intruders would seek entry. From there she smells out the scents of different things that approach the hive.

Foragers are smelled to make sure they are from the colony. Sometimes the worker bee guard will go and scout out the area. In the most alert times, mostly during brooding season, the bee will stand on four legs and let out a warning screech if an intruder comes near. If they continue to come closer they will be stung. After the sting a scent is released which will bring more workers to the area to deal with the intruder.

From there we move on to the executions. Bees will do executions of intruders, robbers, old bees, sick bees, to get rid of drones that are no longer needed, to get rid of unwanted brood be they queens, workers, or drones, and lastly, to help make sure no intruder would want to enter the hive in the first place.

- Gathering Water – Very few people tend to think about the water situation with bees. But it is the job of the worker to go get it for the colony. It's actually one of their most important responsibilities. To get water, bees suck in the moisture through their proboscis. They will get water from any moist area they can and grabbing the water only takes a few seconds.

- Foraging – When the worker bee takes on the role of foraging it also takes on a great many different roles.

- Feeding the Brood – It's important to note that this is different from foraging because it is the actual feeding and not the gathering of food. In fact, this is more in line with the making of food.

- Queen Care – Caring for the queen is another important bee task. The queen is what allows the hive to grow and have a new generation of offspring every year.

- Orientation Flights – This is pretty much a young worker bee only kind of thing. This bee must learn their surroundings so they go on a series of small flights to get acquainted with the surrounding area.

- The Honey Making Process – So this is really a variety of steps and no one bee does all the steps at a time. Bees work in a sort of assembly line.

- Scouting for Areas of Plenty – Bees often have a scout go out to find areas with high concentrations of flowers and nectars and do a dance to show each other where this area is and even how far away.

The Male Drones have a very unique role. They are the breeders. They don't, however, breed with the colony's queen. They go out in search of other colonies to breed with. This insures the health of the bee colony and helps to protect said colonies from certain diseases.

Male drones are genetically identical to the queen bee that laid their egg. This is because male drones are created by the queen laying an unfertilized egg.

Male drones are fed for the first part of their lives. Then it is their job to feed themselves out of the hives stores. Because the drones don't do any foraging themselves, worker bees begin to get irritable of their presence during the winter months.

Their demise comes when the worker bees essentially kick them out as it gets colder so they have enough food to keep the hive alive for winter. The drones go far away from the hive where they eventually die of starvation.

The Queen Bee is technically the official leader of the hive. She is doted on by her subjects and gets the best foods to accommodate her. Her importance is based on her role.

The queen of a hive has the role of laying eggs, both fertilized and unfertilized, for the colony to grow. The worker bees direct her to where she should lay her eggs, but then it is also the queen's duty to expect the comb she is going to and make sure it is completely clean so as to make sure a healthy bee pupa.

The queen bee must fly to a place known as a drone congregation area. These areas are where many drones are drawn to and where queen bees go to get fertilized. These areas are relatively stable over the years and it's a mystical thing how they are located in the same spot year after year and all the drones know where to go, but the only ones who would live long enough to pass on where the area is, is the queen. This is because the drones all die each year.

Also odd, the queen bee only leaves the hive once to mate. That's all she needs. How then is she to know where this drone mating area is? Some studies suggest magnetics might come into play, as male drones who are at least 6 days old have a lot magnetite in their abdomens.

There are some distinguishing features of these mating areas. First, they are about 10-40 meters above ground. Any female flying outside the area is pretty much ignored by the drones. They are located at least 90m from an apiary, and might have a diameter as small as 30 meters, but sometimes the diameter is as large as 200 meters.

It's a big race to mate with the new, virgin queen because then the colony's genetics will be represented. She will gain up to 100 million sperm in her oviducts. Of course, she doesn't use this all at once. The queen stores only about five million sperm in her spermathecal and uses only a few at a time.

If the queen runs out of sperm in her lifetime, she will be replaced with new queen bees.

A queen knows how to determine which eggs are fertilized and which are not. Fertilized eggs turn into females – either workers or queens depending on the food they are given. Unfertilized eggs become male drones. Female worker bees can also create male drones by laying their eggs, which are always unfertilized.

The workers feed royal jelly to all of the eggs for the first two day of their lives. If they need a new queen bee, they may feed a few eggs the royal jelly for the entire larval stage. This is the only difference between the worker females and the fertile queen.

There are three different conditions under which new queen bees are formed.

Swarming

The worker bees create these things called queen cups which they then have their old queen bee lay eggs into. They feed this larva plenty of royal jelly and as soon as they are ready to swarm, they stop feeding the old queen and then seal up the queen cups.

It is now the scout's job to locate a nearby place where the new colony can rest. Usually this is something like a tree. They all rest on the tree for usually no more than hours before moving on to the next intermediary stop. They keep going like this, scouting and moving, until a good place has been found and they start their colony again.

There are still bees left at the nest and so it is their job to decide whether or not they need to allow more than one queen to live. They have prepared about 3 to 5 of them, sometimes more depending on how overcrowded the nest is.

Bees tend to swarm in order to deal with overpopulation and thus the more bees there are, the more subsequent swarms there are. In subsequent swarms, worker bees fly away with virgin queens to repopulate. These queens will later have to go through the mating season.

Swarming tends to happen every second year of a queen's life. In the first year of the queen's life, there is usually very little reason to swarm. The colony is healthy, not overcrowded, and happy.

Supersedure

If the female workers are no longer happy with the queen they will build larger queen cells at the bottom of a frame (usually 6 or more queen cells) whose eggs will start developing in to new queens. The new queen bee will replace the old queen bee.

Female workers may be unhappy with their queen for many reasons. Oftentimes it has to do with her egg laying ability. Females will get rid of queens who have low or no egg laying ability. Sometimes a queen just doesn't make enough eggs. This is very bad for the hive because if they can't grow they are more likely to become sick or overrun with intruders and thieves.

Other times females will get rid of a queen because she has run out of sperm. It is the queen's job to make sure she has enough sperm from the mating to last for her entire life. Failure to do so harms the entire colony as she will then only be able to make drones. Because of this, the colony would suffer.

When a colony is not happy with the current queen and have decided to replace her; that is when supersedure happens. When the new queen hatches, the old one is executed or pushed out.

An Emergency Queen

Sometimes a queen bee will suddenly die or be killed. When this happens it is drastically important for the worker bees to make a new queen or their entire colony will suffer.

If a queen bee suddenly dies or is accidentally killed, the female worker bees will quickly notice the lack of a queen pheromone. The can sense this very easily. They then quickly kick in to motion the production of an emergency queen.

The workers will select recently laid eggs from the old queen and start feeding them additional Royal Jelly. If the bees are lucky, these eggs will have been from two days ago or less. These eggs that are being fed the royal jelly will start developing in to queen bees, thus saving the colony from certain death.

This is also why worker bees are given the ability to make an egg into a queen instead of a worker. Without this trait, there would be many more bee deaths and much less honey.

As stated before, the only difference between a worker bee female and a queen bee is what they are fed. Males only come from unfertilized eggs, but all females come from the same kind of fertilized egg.

When a worker bee wants another worker bee, they stop feeding them the jelly after the two day mark. But when a worker bee wants a queen bee, either for swarming, supersedure, or in an emergency, all they have to do is continue to give the little bee larva the royal jelly.

Royal jelly production starts in the heads of the worker bees and is secreted into the queen bee cells. It is about 67% water, but contains a lot of sugars, enzymes, and vitamins. Queen bees tend to have their comb completely stocked full of the jelly, more than they can eat. This lets the larva know to develop general queen morphology such as the bigger, linger, sleek body and the fully functional ovaries to lay eggs.

THE NEW QUEEN BEE

There can never be two queen bees in the same hive. The bees will try to kill each other. This even counts for new queens. New queen bees will even sting the other queen bee larva as soon as they hatch. The first queen to hatch is the new queen and she kills the un-hatched queens by stinging them through the walls of their cells.

A queen's life cycle is pretty much 3 days of being an egg, five days of being a larva and having her cell capped starting at day 7. Next she has about a week of being a pupa before she finally emerges from her capped cell.

Mating

The next four days are all about mating. The new queen goes on what is known as her nuptial flight. This is when she goes from being a virgin queen who secretes pheromones to a fully-fledged and fertilized egg laying queen.

The new queen flies to the drone area. It is unsure how she knows how to get there as it is only the drones that have the magnetite in their abdomen.

She finds the area which is 10 to 40 meters off the ground and now it is her duty to stay within the area of the ritual so that she can mate with as many drones as she can. A queen typically mates with about 10 to 20 drones. These drones can mate with less than 10 queens because their sex actually gets ripped off of their bodies in many instances. Many male drones don't survive the mating season.

Of course, only about one in every thousand male drone bees even get the chance to mate with one queen. And even if a mated male did get past the mating season alive, his colony would shun him because he has done his duty.

So the queen mates with about twenty drones, but these drones are as different from one another as possible. It is best for the queen bee to get as much genetic variation as possible to make sure her colony stays healthy.

She'll go for different traits in her mates. She'll look for pollen collecting, flying longer distances, cleaning cells, carrying heavier workloads. She'll basically be breeding for the continued survival of her group.

In fact, if it is found that the queen has mated with a drone from their own colony, the worker bees will kill those emerging larva because they are not good at all for the health of the hive.

The New Queen Take Over

The new queen, after mating with as many males as she can and getting a diverse amount of sperm, returns to the nest and begins to lay eggs. She is immediately accepted by the other bees and life resumes as usual after the old queen leaves.

It's at this time that the hive then swarms and the old queen leaves with some of the worker bees to make a new colony in a different area.

All bee eggs that the new queen lays will hatch after about three and a half days. From there, times begin to vary in the rest of the process. You can figure out how old any non-emerged bee is by the state of the capped or uncapped top.

The new queen bee tends not to have any problems. Problems may begin to happen if the colony realizes the new queen is weak or has taken on their own drones as mates. This kind of problem is very serious for the workers and so they would make a new queen and do a supersedure of some sort.

Otherwise the queen bee has full rule of the hive until her pheromone secretion is missing or they decide to swarm again. This usually will happen in the second year of the queen bee's rule.

FORMING A NEW COLONY

After the queen bee moves or dies, changes happen and oftentimes new colonies are formed. New colonies are formed from some of the remaining bees and either a new virgin queen or an older queen as seen in swarming.

Swarming

Swarming is the most common reason why a new colony might form. It is the bees way of moving to a new location.

Now there is a distinct difference in swarming and something known as absconding. Absconding is something that only African honey bees do. African honey bees are a lot different and more aggressive than the European honey bees.

If a hive absconds, it is an African honey bee colony. However, African honey bees also swarm. It's important to know the difference though, as European honey bees who are the most common honey bee and the ones that beekeepers prefer, only swarm.

Absconding is where the entire hive gets up and goes. No bees are left, no larva. There is nothing left behind. Some people think that absconding is part of the reason African honey bees are less susceptible to colony collapse.

Swarming on the other hand involves only some of the bees leaving. This is often due to overcrowding in the hive. When there are too many bees in a colony, they make some new queen eggs, nurture them, and then a lot of the colony leaves with the old queen for a new place.

Sometimes there are many swarms that leave. The ones that don't leave with the old queen leave with virgin queens who will then have to participate in the mating system in order to be able to create fertilized eggs. Even after various swarms leave the hive, part of the original group are left. With a virgin queen.

Bee Dancing

In the formation of new colonies as well as when finding food, water and other resources, bees have a unique way of communicating. While bees make sounds, they can also "talk" with scent. More unique than that though is their movements.

Honey bees may communicate with what we humans call a dance.

They use this dance for two main uses. The first use for their elaborate dance is in foraging. They move around and seemingly point in certain directions to let other bees know where good supplies like nectar, pollen, or water might be found.

The honey bees use two primary types of dances to communicate these thing. These are the wiggle dance and the circle dance. The circle dance, as the name kind of suggests, is where the honey bee moves in a circular motion. This is to note that a kind of food is within 50 meters from where the hive is located.

The second kind of dance, the wiggle dance, is a little bit more complex. This dance involves a kind of doubled/crossed circle motion like a figure eight, plus a little wiggle in the abdomen. The meaning of the wiggle dance is similar to the circular dance, basically how far away the food source is. Instead of being close, however, the wiggle dance indicates food is over 150 meters away. The longer a bee dances, the further away the food happens to be.

Dancing bees can also show what direction a food might be in. To do this, the bee does the wiggle dance and promptly moves itself towards the direction of the vertical positioning of the sun. While this sounds complicated, it's actually rather simple and effective for the group.

This kind of communication is important to know even, and especially, in newer colonies.

THE LIFE CYCLE OF THE BEE

Bees are amazing creatures and as was already mentioned, they go through a variety of changes. From an egg to an invertebrate insect, many things happen to the honey bee in its life.

Young honey bees start their life much the same as humans do. They are unfertilized eggs in the reproductive system of their mother, and they need sperm in order to become a fertilized egg. Well, that's only partially true.

You see, only the female honey bees have to come from an unfertilized egg. And the only mother that can make female babies is the colonies queen. Every other female honey bee in the hive is infertile and can only make unfertilized eggs. The queen can also make unfertilized eggs.

An unfertilized egg is how a male honey bee is born, a fertilized egg is how a female honey bee is born. From there, everything else is decided based on what happens after they hatch.

From Larvae to Death

After almost exactly three and a half days, every kind of egg – both the fertilized and the unfertilized – hatches into a little tiny baby. These babies are called larva. These tiny larva lay in the comb that they were hatched in.

The adult worker bees in the hive tend to the needs of the tiny larva. The larva eats mainly pollen and honey, and so the adult workers feed them that for about three weeks. Of course, larva doesn't just suddenly become an adult bee.

After about four more days the little babies become pupa, which is similar to their larvae state. They are still fed a continuous supply of honey and pollen, except for the queen bee babies who are the exception. They get a special concoction called royal jelly.

All bees get royal jelly for the first two days of hatching, but queen larva get fed copious amounts to help them grow into special, fertile, queen bees.

At a certain point the pupa get their combs capped, or covered with beeswax. Each kind of bee gets capped at a slightly different time. Queen bees get capped as early as possible, usually within seven and a half to eight days. This is partially to try to make sure that they don't kill their fellow queens, in case the hive plans on swarming.

Worker bees get capped on about day nine. Finally, drone bees which are the male bees and came from the unfertilized eggs, they get capped on day ten.

Lastly, the now mature bees escape from their capped combs by chewing themselves out. Again, each bee leaves his or her comb at a varying time. Queen bees, the ones who were fed lots of royal jelly, emerge on day sixteen, which is a little over a week after her cell was capped. After another approximately twelve days, this bee may start laying eggs, since within those twelve days she has hopefully participated in the mating ceremony.

After the queen comes the female worker bee. These honey bees emerge after about ten or eleven days from having her beeswax comb sealed. Luckily, these infertile honey bees do not have to fight with one another like the queen bees and thus the first thing they do is clean up the comb they just emerged from.

After another twenty or so days, the female worker bee can begin foraging. But before then her duty is cleaning up cells and looking after the other young hatchlings.

After the female worker bee comes the male drone. Male drone honey bees emerge an entire two weeks after their cells were capped by the adult worker bees. Some speculate that they take so long to grow and mature in order to conserve the hives food production.

In fact, in just another two weeks these drones begin to fly towards the mating area known as the drone congregation area. This is where their lives are much different from those of other bees. A drone's purpose is to mate with as many queens as they can before they end up dying from basically having their abdomen ripped out in the process of said mating.

Only about 1 in every thousand male drones mates during the season. Those that mated and survived are shunned from their colonies. Those that, in fact, could not mate are tolerated in the hive for perhaps a while longer before the weather gets too cold.

Once the weather is cold, the drones are sent to starve.

Grown Worker Bees

Let's look back at the worker bee's life. As stated, the first thing a worker bee does when she emerges from her cell is, well, to work. By cleaning her comb she in a way signals that she is ready to take on all the responsibilities of any other full grown adult female worker honey bee.

The more a worker bee matures the more responsibility it has. That's why foraging is seen as one of the biggest responsibilities... it's the furthest from the hive.

At the beginning of a worker bee's life they start by cleaning and caring for the young. They tend to the larva by secreting a kind of liquid from their abdominal glands. They start to become responsible for carrying the items brought by the foragers. Then they are in charge of storing the food. Soon they are scouting and starting to get acclimated to the surrounding area.

Young worker bees actually spend a couple days doing what are known as orientation flights so that they don't get lost when it's finally time for them to go out in search of food and, even more important, water.

A worker bee's responsibility include cleaning cells, clearing debris from the hive, capping the cells of the pupa when they're supposed to, tending to the brood, attending to the needs of the queen, receiving nectar from the forages, storing food, packing pollen, building the honey comb out of beeswax, going on orientation flights, guarding the hive from any intruders or thieves, and foraging for life necessities like food or water.

In terms of work habits, worker bees are the most incredible workers known to man. They work day in and day out, they care for one another, the clean, they make sure there's enough food with even a surplus, and they seem to enjoy themselves.

In terms of food habits, adult full grown bees eat mostly pollen and nectar. There is always enough to go around.

ABOUT THE AUTHOR

Lil Wolfie is a Pseudonym used for a series of books and eBooks on a variety of subjects. The person behind this pseudonym wishes not to be made known for reasons including family, friends, work, and other related reasons.

www.ingramcontent.com/pod-product-compliance
Lightning Source LLC
Chambersburg PA
CBHW070456290526
45791CB00005B/2134